Liminal

Poems by Bill Burtis

NINE MILE BOOKS

Publisher: Nine Mile Art Corp.
Editors: Bob Herz, Stephen Kuusisto, Andrea Scarpino
Art Editor Emeritus: Whitney Daniels
Cover Art: Photo by Bill Burtis
Photo of the author by Nancy Jean Hill.

Nine Mile Books is an imprint of Nine Mile Art Corp.

The publishers gratefully acknowledge support of the New York State
Council on the Arts with the support of Governor Andrew M. Cuomo
and the New York State Legislature. We also acknowledge support of
the County of Onondaga and CNY Arts through the Tier Three Project
Support Grant Program. We have also received significant support from
the Central New York Community Foundation. This publication would
not have been possible without the generous support of these groups.
We are very grateful to them all.

ISBN: 978-1-7354463-7-0

Acknowledgements

My gratitude to the members of City Hall Poets for years of invaluable workshopping; to Kimberly Cloutier-Green, Bob Herz, Lesley Kimball, Stephen Kuusisto, Bill Schulz and especially Nancy Jean Hill, fine poets all, for their advice, edits, humor and inspiration; to Jim Crenner for just about everything.

Some of the poems included here have appeared in the following publications or online journals:

Aurorean: *Peepers*
Aspen Anthology: *View from a Third Story Window on a Winter Afternoon; The Woodsman*
Chelsea: *The Bat Hunter*
Good Fat: *Walking the Climate Scientists Dog*
Nine Mile: *At the Fair; History*
Paris Review: *Acapulco Rubric*
Poet Showcase: An Anthology of New Hampshire Poets: *Chase*
Port *Smith*: *Cellar Hole; Apple Seed*
Rat's Ass Review: *Ballad of the Blue Piano; Owl*
Seneca Review: *Why You Have Never Heard of Me Before; Dawn Comes to the All-Night Diner*
The Shore: *Hubble Ultra Deep Field Image; After the Last Train*
Sou'wester: *The Last Weekend in the Country*
Three Quarter Review: *Coyotes*
Tower Journal: *Summer Night; Turquoise; With Without*

Earlier versions of several of these poems were included in a chapbook, *Villains*, published by W. D. Hoffstadt & Sons.

Table of Contents

Liminal

for Martine, Lily, and Liam

I

The Nature of Angels

If there were an angel on the stairs
you would not move aside.

An angel on a bicycle
flickers like sunlight on wavelets.

An angel does not remember
where it came from, but longs to return.

The thought running along the edge
of your consciousness is a signal shard

of angel radio. You suppose
you know no angels.

When you have wandered out of the storm,
an angel is leaving.

It is in the nature of angels
not to show their wings.

All Off

The man in the middle of the street is crying.
Even from this distance,
at which you cannot see the tears
you can see that his body has the warp
of someone who is crying. He is no less a man
for this crying: see the scraps of life
blowing around him and the way
the sunlight trembles in the smoke.

His loss is imaginable to any of us
who have seen him and this street before,
heard the sirens or radio crackle that are
its best explication. But we do not imagine
this crying man's tomorrow, the days
and days, their crumpled hollowness.

That is left in the dust of the news cycle, the wheels
of the plane folding into its belly, the world moving onward
with the camera crew, removed with a touch
of the button on the remote: All off, all gone.

Dawn Comes to the All-Night Diner
for John Bowie

The man we think of here, face sallow,
dark in its depths from the shadow
cast by the low fedora's brim,
raises a hand to his forehead, the dull
ache of the neon, endless cup of coffee.
Only it does come, preceded by shades
of lilac, throwing its wash
across the dirty windows, making
the waitress yawn, the cook
look up from the sports and shift
against the stainless ice cream case.
And then everything is still again,
but in a white light.

A meager attempt. Hopper had these colors
absolutely. Truth is, Bowie, the place
might have been empty: you spent half your time
behind the camera in your attempt to record this—
or cartoon, slander and forget it.
I have no questions about that.

Someone enters, straddles a stool;
two more come in; the juke box wakes
and stretches the first notes of some lament.
This part is all Midwestern, the sun
making the truckers hungry; in the city,
it's hookers, subway people....

You leave. A steam whistle blows and you
jerk your head up, watching the white smoke
shooting against the blue sky just
out of sync with its music. Now you turn,
heavily, and begin to move off,
but toward the camera, left, growing
larger, largest just before you disappear.

Villains

We are part of the sleeper's dreams.
Still with us, he nearly wakes,

not knowing what he listens for:
the distance of sounds at night,

their ticking precision; rooms of the house,
silent with possibilities, shadows, appear.

Slowly, the sleeper returns
to a different landscape

with the dark of valleys at dawn, a light
hard as metal. Someone walks out in it:

his breath shows in the cold, tracks in the frost.
In the barn, a pickup sputters, starts.

We can imagine the next instant: the truck appears,
the driver swings the big doors closed, drives off ...

But we may be deprived of this, what comes next,
forced to imagine what lies ahead for this driver

and what he's left behind. The sun rises,
the sleeper wakes, trying to remember

something that almost occurs, but fails,
leaving a space

filled by the recitations of bystanders,
the false evidence of those who arrived too late.

We can see, oh, a few clouds, fields,
an ambulance raising dust up the road.

Walking the Climate Scientist's Dog
for Cameron Wake

Wyeth has no concern
for the environmental impact
of his earnest waterings
as he expands his sphere of influence.
Inside, his master points out
the sure curve of ours, how
nature has begun to notice
our comings and goings far more
than those of others.

Outside, I marvel
at this dog's doggedness –
as if he would find no dish
nor anyone home willing
to feed him, draw water.
Or perhaps his ear, being closer
to the ground, hears
a message we have now forgotten:
"It's good to stay in practice."

Three decades ago, I walked
from boundary tree to marker,
stepping off 40 acres, plus
or minus, enough, anyway
to heat a house and fill
a winter's worth of stomachs.
How odd to think what was
all the rage then is now
seeming merely practical

more like the twisting
in the trunk of the white oak
weaving its way to sunlight
or Wyeth's persistent stretching
at this leather leash to mark off
a scrap of earth sufficient
to keep him in all his ways.

What silly animals we are
who watch in wonder the sunlit cloud top

and assume any nuance in nature.

On the Timely Death of Literature
after James Wright

"Literature is dead—just in time."
–James Crenner, 1938 –

The bronze butterfly is asleep again
here, where I have borrowed it.
The meadow is filled with people.
On a catafalque of golden stones
the casket is opened, revealing,
for an instant, a figure, radiant
and fair as remorse. Then
in the evening sunlight
there are flowers and great, splendid
moths that rise like darkness
above the empty field.

Later, the hawk returns
with word of snow: tomorrow
the leaves will be gone
brown angels flying before the wind
that tosses the empty hammock.

Three Yellow Balloons

Would have gone unnoticed
but for the ball of fire.

Except we watched the scene unfold
over and over and there, look

there they are, moments before
coming up the street, bobbing

on their invisible strings
above the crowd, above the heads

of the bombers. Who was it held them?
A child, happy for three balloons

bright as the April sun? A parent
unable to overcome the need

to keep this child from the sorrow
of a sunny balloon lost

into the blue, blue sky?
Or were these the gift intended

to greet the runner
crossing that finish line?

No matter. They are history now,
rising out of the soot gray billow

of the child's sorrow
of the runner's end

of the smoke that punched up
and then tattered and swirled away

into the air above the street
as bomb smoke always does.

The Rest of Us

It's O.K. for the rich and the lucky to keep still;
no one wants to know about them anyway.
   –Rilke (trans: Robert Bly)

But the rest of us? Keep moving,
even if it's only rolling side to side
in the old creaking springs of our beds.
Keep moving, believing we are
gathering speed toward transformation
as if we were the particles
physicists search for, as if we, too,
could be in two places at once—
our mother's arms and at the bank
receiving big bills in fistfuls we take
down the street, flinging them around
like leaflets or the fake tickets
the barkers hand out when the circus
comes to town to make you think you're getting
a great deal when really, really, you are
not going to see so much as a monkey
on a unicycle and when you turn around to leave
even the big top is gone, mother like distant smoke
and there's just this muddy field to make you
think that some part of this must have been
true but the only thing that mattered
was the singing, the harmony of many,
many voices that you missed entirely.

Quasimodo

From the glistening white tower
of the cinder block closet
in the center of the self-service gas station
he emerges, hunched,
a bristled stand of red hair,
a cast eye he rolls toward me
as if to say, as he slams the door,
keys clinking, that he is master
of this keep, this sanctum whose
dials and levers control the flow
of thousands of gallons
of immensely flammable fluid.

He shuffles off to help
another hapless soul
whose card will not scan,
whose hose will not stretch,
whose gas cap will not twist loose,
idly scratching inside
filth-blackened Dickies
as he limps grossly, grunting
to the outer island, peering back occasionally
as if to insure I'd not left
my vehicle unattended.

He lives in the asbestos-sided
one-bedroom cape shoved against the chain fences
protecting interstate highways from wildlife,
a neighborhood of bent antennas lit
by the eerie orange street lamps that stand watch
over another planet in an alternative universe
where I arrived a few years after birth,
left there by some miraculously
minor slight offhandedly committed,
resulting in a form, bent by the wind of insult,
the wringing hand of anger,
so despicable it could only be kept

locked in a white dungeon
surrounded by a moat of flame.

Why You Have Never Heard of Me Before

"Pourquoi écrire, et pour qui?" – Louis Aragon

because, on childhood's rainy days,
I never wondered about brothers or sisters,
but was content to fight small, plastic wars
on the battlefield of my bedroom floor,
and left the sandbox late in life.

because, even now, with so much life
forgotten, I like my private battles best,
and prefer to live in countrysides
among quaint, honest people in a traditional dress
which I have either remembered or made up.

because no one they know is ever listed there,
and they are all the town has for history,
the people love the fragile casualty lists
I post on the white stone walls of the houses,
and I am a happy and an almost holy man.

Stopover

I remember it, a great Cape barn
of a house, west of Boston,
a stop on the Underground Railway.

Inside, under the mossy beams
and the aroma of raw wood polished
with centuries of human oil,

below the black peat of the hearths,
were the dirt-floored stalls. They filled
my senses with ferns and humus

a smoke that hunched against the damp stone walls.

The house was red, at ease in the fired
veins of autumn; a spider's perfect web, full
of dewy prisms in a sunlit eave.

But mostly, I remember the basement,
the breathing that went on.

Reading Before Sleep

Offering this incense of other lives,
wrapping myself in these sheets,
to be mailed in someone else's letter,
I exceed the day and stop
just beyond the part
that carries me toward dreams.

In the moment after the book is closed,
but still standing between my hands,
the prayer itself, over my heart,
which is falling then
in the downdraft, falling
in the shaft, the dark chimney
where anyone like you used to be.

And falling, I remember—
flying, rising like the birds' songs,
mounting without effort, those melodies
up out of the trees like light, slowly at first
and then filling the world so loudly
we cannot sleep—what
is holding still and what is turning,
my own wings spread
I begin the curve slowly upwards,

bring the book to its place beneath the light,
let my hand switch on the darkness
without knowing I have
done any of these things
the way love exists or its
graceful, thoughtless expression.

Signal Loss

Skiing alone in New Hampshire's February woods,
I hear the ringtone assigned my oldest daughter
from the cell phone in my pack, calling
from the northern edge of the Sahara,
the darkness of space threading in her voice,
stitched there by some satellite's bristling antennae.
She says no, it is only the rustling
curtain of dusk falling rain-like
across the cooling sand. I think
these are miracles beyond technology.

Years later on the deck by the river, a Skype call.
She is visible, walking home in Istanbul,
where lights in the street
and the many-tongued crowds
whirl and spin in the handheld image
of her walking, the sound of her voice
clear as near, her face in its electronic
incarnations, moving in and out with her stride.
And then a graying, ghostly mélange
of light, her voice suddenly curving
and twisting in the ethereal
distances. I ask what happened, she
says I am walking beside the wall.

What wall? I ask. A silence and she,
forgiving: The wall, Dad. It surrounds the city."
Then the signal is lost beyond the stonework
of emperors, unbreached by centuries of marauders.
What was left was blackness and silence
deep in a universe swirling.

December

The light of big store windows
spills onto the damp faces
of shoppers pushing their way
through a mild sleet.
In the foreground, a man's
silhouette, hatless, bent
as if he'd lost something
on the shining pavement,
or bad news a moment ago
is now running its sharp edge
across the throat of all
the days he can imagine.

A moment later, he lifts his face
and in the firelight-orange
window glare, it is impossible
to tell if it is streaked
by tears or sleet. His hands,
empty in his pockets,
find only air as soft as ash.
He stands for a moment,
knowing everything he loves
is as far from him now
as the dusty chorus of crickets
just past the sunset
of a summer night.

Coyotes

On a cracking cold full-moon night
I clamp on skis and glide
out across the solid reservoir
before tracking up the pure
moon-pearl slope of snowfield
toward the dark curtain of trees
and stop just short of the woods.
Warmed in the climb, I survey the pale landscape
the few intrepid stars glimmering
through the mixed radiance of snow
and lunar light, unclamp and lay down
to wriggle a warm angel in the snow.

I know this is the last of the rules
I should be breaking on a winter night.
But I am warm, the sky rewarding,
and I do drift off to sleep, perhaps to freeze
but anyway to dream of rooms full of firelight
where people in large furs talk of wolves,
how they sniff and drool in growling circles
before they attack and one woman shows
how it's done, sidling around the room,
sniffing up to each ear and finally
up to mine, at which I almost wake
and feel in half dream the slight warmth
of wet breath on my cheek
and lie long moments coming to until I know
something is sniffing at my ear.

I jump from my angel yelling. The shout
bounces off the frozen water and trees and I see
three, four or more thin-bellied frames fly
off through swirls of snow
into the shadows of the woods.
Around me, their paw prints
pock and pack the snow.
I shiver and look hard for eyes
in the blackest spaces between trees

before bending to retrieve my skis
and poles and push off
down the hill toward home.

Diving into the Moon
for M

Down close to the water
where Bennett Road runs tight along the river
is an outcrop of granite colored by all that earth
and wind and water have to offer. It is easy to miss,
darker than the deep tea color of the river
descending into blackness below sunlight.

It used to be invisible from the road before floods
took away roadside alder and other scrub.
Friends and I would skinny dip there, sleek
young bodies plunging five feet into the cool flow
where the bending river swept against rock
and steep bank, hidden from passersby.

And one night I took you there, surprised at how easily
you escaped the chrysalis of your clothing, emerging
white and lithe in the moonlight. We stood together
staring into darkness, only ripples sparkling briefly below
and you, suddenly grasping my arm, as if forgetting
our nakedness, breathed on my shoulder

"How do we get in?" It was impossible to describe
any arc that would carry you safely to where I knew
the river was deep enough to accept us. But then
it was there, a wavering, pale yellow circle,
the landing place. I slid my arm around your waist
and drew closer, pointing: "Dive into the moon."

And you did, the long paleness of your body
a tracer from rock to an explosion of white water
and then you emerged again, with a whoop and laughing.
I remember how delighted I was you'd trusted me
enough to take that dive into the black water, but perhaps
you did not place your faith in me, but in the moon.

Acapulco Rubric

The contemplation of horrors is not edifying;
neither does it strengthen the soul.
—Anthony Hecht, *Rites and Ceremonies*

At one time, under this same title,
I told the whole story of the kidnapped girl
and her Mexican tortures.
It was intended to teach everyone a lesson.
But now…well, let me be brief:

The local police once invited a friend
to take a peek at some confiscated skin flicks
and accidentally treated him to a real horror
in which a young white girl, evidently American,
is chained to a wall while

rough hands wait
for the pink flames of her nipples to rise
into the hot, ready mouths of pliers.
The whip begins, tearing her
mother-and-father white flanks open for the camera,
and she goes limp in the final arms of her vacation,
mumbles into telephones, gives up urine like a flag….

But enough. Suffice it to say
she was beautiful and brought sensationally to death
for the fat black-market money of impotent old men,
and that my friend was mercilessly badgered
by those in the bar, and told the whole story.

And I wrote it down, feeling that—but what does it matter?
I guess it had a message,
that no good comes from telling bad stories.

Standing in the Woods

Standing in the woods, somewhere out of bounds,
I recall the moment of becoming overcome
by a bodily uncertainty, the trees shifting as if by plan,
moving just slightly to one side or the other,
the path gone, a wisp of ground fog in sunlight.

I remember Steven Snow explaining "sees"—the means
to direct a woodsman in an unmapped, sign-less way,
memory of as far as you can see leading him, making
the next turn or marker three sees down a woodland track.

One is a way of being lost, the other a kind of faith,
pretending you know the direction of salvation.
And the old men's talk of being in the woods
is fresh as smoke or the sound of a gun, something
that can only be itself, a certain thing.

And so today, standing in the woods is the best I can do:
breathing in the scent of the woods, its own damp breath,
I can imagine daughters safe in streets foreign and urban,
my son aglow with purpose and as much desire
as the young ought to be allowed.

II

The Bat Hunter

A bat has eight fingers and loose thumbs.
When you hit a bat,
the wings clench like fists:
three small stones hit the ground at once.
When the bat hunter finds him,
the brittle wings still row with his breathing.

As he kneels to hear this dream of death,
the boy is pure sound in the pale evening sky.
Down the street, a dog howls.
In the hutch, his mother's china
quivers into a corner.

The blind, black eyes shine
like jewels in the velvet skin,
stare down the gleaming, raised barrels
to the eyes of the hunter.

Hard, glistening, man-like eyes.

Swimming before Sunrise

I pull the moon slowly from her bed
high in the shoreline hemlocks.

The quarrels of the crows continue
variously with worry and accord

all lost to me, on my back, listening
only to the rustle of the water sweeping by.

I swim out past where I can see
the tops of the tallest pines.

Soon the silhouettes of pines on the island
rise against the color blooming in the eastern sky.

The moon is far adrift now; I turn
and with an earnest stroke, drive her slowly back .

to nest between the pointed caps of hemlock.
I grasp the cold steel of the ladder and realize

a whole year's turning must pass
before the moon again waits

between these trees at this hour,
a precision unmatched by any human measure.

The loons call, announcing presence
and loss, presence and loss.

The Ballad of the Blue Piano

Two girls in the neighborhood made me
a barter, really, where a glimpse
of my bald genitalia bought
a view of their strange blankness.

It happened several times in a playhouse
until I refused them after having a dream:
a small boy, in a place with the cracked
barrenness of a dead lake, whimpers

and tries vainly to raise his crumpled pants
above his knees; there was a thin light,
as of sun through dust. The dream, of course,
was not mine alone, though I thought so long enough

to develop a passionate insecurity.
Women have their own reasons for alcohol
and silence, but this vision stands between men
when they try honestly to speak to one another.

It is in the throat of that boy that the words stick.

I have had two other dreams like that,
both waking: one on a cold day
in a forest, young and full of the damp
smell of fertility, where I found

the remains of an orchard, a single tree
whose yellow apples shone
like gold cast to rot in the decaying
mouths of dead leaves.

The other has more history.
Against the sagging railing of a junk house
rested a piano, an old upright,
painted blue. A blue piano.

Inside, a girl played Chopin
without sheet music, her fingers
slender dancers. She sees me, nods,
and goes on for the rest of the summer.

Somebody Else's Shoes
for Liam

When I cleaned out the house
where my parents lived for 25 years
I found a pair of Docksiders
on a shelf above the basement stairs.
They looked right, and when I
slipped them on still tied, they fit.

I wondered whose they were
because since I was a child I'd thought
my father's feet were bigger than mine
and my mother's so much smaller—
not to mention she'd have worn
a grass skirt sooner than Docksiders.

I meant to ask. Instead I learned
that things known too long
may not be known at all. I found
Death sleeps with one eye half open, his teeth
resting gently on his lower lip.
He does not walk the streets,

and his shoes are the white of light
seen through the avalanche,
the white the angels use to convince us.
Finally, bending to kiss him, I stop,
lips a breath away, feeling the cold.
None of this is expected.

View from a Third Story Window on a Winter Afternoon

"Sometimes at night I light a lamp so as not to see." – Antonio Porcia

I am looking over the roofs of Dover,
New Hampshire, listening to the children
on their sleds below the empty trees
on the icy bank of the railway.

It is impossible to decipher the language
they are speaking, the way
the song the orchestra will play
is lost in all its pieces
until the instruments find their tune.

There are things that turn
against us without meaning to.
Look at the fathers. Listen
as their children try to speak.

After the Last Train

In the old ceramic subway hall,
too early or late in the day, never
any weather but the storms
brought in and out by trains,

one now just sifting down
behind the departure
of the last train, the one
the man has missed,

he rocks uncertainly
heel to toe, hands pocketed,
listening, noticing again
the blunt brown smell

of a place so long
without sunlight, full
of used breath and skin dust
and earth filling in.

Here there is, too,
a palpable waiting of souls,
left by so many eyes
peering into the tunnel,

having felt the push of air,
to see the shine on the curving wall,
hear the first faint clicking,
feel the slow thunder in their feet.

But he knows none of that is coming,
sees the next hours same as this one.
After a while, he will turn to the stairs
for solace, for the change and direction they offer.

Kinsman

An old white dog
lies on the warm gray
driveway stones
in this morning's sun.
How old he is
you cannot tell,
the grizzle of his muzzle
hidden by his general whiteness.
But I know him to be
my elder brother by his
perfect surrender, to which
I now aspire, but with reluctance,
the unwillingness of the mind
to succumb to gravity,
knowing where this settling goes.
Today I will perhaps try
to follow an old dog's lead,
forego the hike or bike ride into town
and wait here on the western porch
for the sun to come around.

Owl

When the owl leaves the branch, he becomes
the wind and the soundless dark,
threads the hem of branches with a faith
before knowledge, safe in the space between things.

There is a boy running through hemlocks
faster than he can think, out on the windy edge
where he is only his body moving, not conscious
of the rough bark, the whole hurt of a tree.

He makes no sound, breathes
between the pounding pulses of his heart
and his feet. Flying over
the crest of a rocky hillock, he slows

slightly out of fear
not that he will hit anything or fall,
but that he will leave the earth
and the company of his kind.

Still

Most of the time the sheets are already on
when I get there, lugging my little Yashika and notepad.
Even when there is no blood, you know a body
by the familiar rhythm of noses, knees and toes: dead human.

One time, I arrived at a scene of scattered auto parts
and a sheet was up in a tree like a Halloween decoration.
There were sheets inside cars; sometimes parts of the bodies
had escaped and the cops would be hunting around like kids at Easter.

This day, he was gone already, sheet and all,
into the back of the ambulance pulling soundlessly away.
Workmen in darkened T-shirts clustered, slumped shoulders
the definition of sadness in the white afternoon light.

A cop told me the victim's name, an Italian name, his age,
and that he was hit by a steamroller, gesturing into the empty space,
equidistant from me and the cop, the machine and the murmuring
groups of workers, whose talking stopped then. Their eyes

drifted silently from me to the spot where a small white object
shown against the dirt. I walked over. A few inches
from a bright pool of blood congealing toward crimson
lay a crumpled unfiltered cigarette, still smoking.

Room Full of Fog, San Francisco

At the top of the last flight of stairs at the top of the Sunset
I had a little room, a cupola big enough for a small bed
and a few dreams. Evenings were often crowded
with orange light; mornings shrouded in Pacific cloud,
the rooftop, the hills and contorted pines, gone.

Sometimes the fog poured through the streets, cotton lava,
washing away everything lapping at my window sills.
I could step out onto the roof, ankle-deep in the wispy coolness,
into a blue-skied, sunny world all my own,
the vague sounds of a lost city muffling below.

One night, late under the orange blanket of the streetlit swirling fog,
I came home and climbed slowly, aware as I rose to the landing
five steps below my room, of the cold, the air that ran on my skin.
When I turned on the light, there was a sudden diaphanous yellow,
an utter heaven, the room replaced entirely by cloud,

bed, lamp, dresser, erased as if only the dreams remained
as a ghostly incandescence into which I reached
for any surface that would tell me I was still
here, holding a place, having not succeeded
in a way unintended, entirely too soon.

White Pine

On an October day, my daughters and son chirping around me,
minds quick as the mouths of baby birds: Why are the hickories
and beeches gold, birches bright as lemons, the maples gaudy?

These are the true colors of trees, the eldest states,
the rest of the year hidden—like the stars—by too much sunlight.
But with a sudden sadness she questions the yellowing of the pines,
a sure sign, she says, of bad air, bad water, bad things. But I

strike a familiar pose, finger raised in protest against bad things and,
taking a sprig of pine, I show them what my science-teacher father
showed me: the deep green needles at the tip, followed by a scar,
followed by another year of green, another scar and then

this oldest now-brown year of needles, how they drop off dry,
mimic the whole tree, the lowest branches, brittle and barren,
breaking off, making room—and they are amazed I am this wise.
But I confess I know this only because my father told me and that
someday they will tell their children. Perhaps because she knows

how families are trees, this eldest, wisest daughter looks
through my words, past the scars, into my heart, and then away.

At the Aquarium

A hammerhead swims close to the immense, clear wall,
the eye on the nearest lobe of its terrible, eons-old head
pivoting at the boy of six or seven who has suctioned himself
against this window with as much of his flesh as he can mold
to it, his own starfish, to become a part of that other world.

He is breaking the rules, of course, but against what monstrous
rule breaking, the capture indoors of an ocean, can we measure
what is clearly only enthusiasm, a child's desire to be in there
swimming with this kaleidoscope of languid harmony, the wing
of the gliding ray, the mighty pulse of the blue fin, or the idle

power of the tiger shark, its effortless thread of the water?
What failure of our nature could fault this child's desire
to touch, to feel, perhaps to ride, these utterly other creatures,
to be one? I can see the glass beginning its transubstantiation,
its slow surrender to the boy's warmth and eagerness,

how it bends at each point of pressure to begin to admit him
and I wonder whether he will become a fish, another creature
entirely, or if he will simply learn to breathe underwater, and
I am about to connect this with my own speculation about crossing
over, how much will be gained and how much will be lost,

when his mother, coming suddenly as if from a great distance
out of her own Piscean reverie, registers the calamity of the wall
surrendering, whether to admit her son or to disgorge suddenly
the twitching, snapping mass upon him I cannot say, but her eyes
and voice convey a terror commensurate only with the latter.

Waning Gibbous

This morning on my back, plying slowly
through the small waves of this northern pond,
the diaphanous fingernail is a vessel
full to burgeoning, inviting me to feel
the soft weight, the paunch
of my experience, its blue bulge
the sack full of all I am.

The pale crescent then becomes
the leading edge of the rest of my days,
a heat shield to be burned away
by the flaring fervor, the thickness of life.
And I swim on, happy there is now no loss
nor gain, but just this movement, phase on phase
across the wondrous sky.

Chase
for Martine

1.
One day, leaving the park
by the ocean beach, I looked
up from installing your sister
in her car seat to see you
running toward the park gate,
arms outstretched, after a car
that looked like ours.

I knew everything at once—
what you believed, your spirit
like you, bent and staggered by your tears.

2.
Today, a boy that small, three perhaps,
still young enough that his intention to run
outdistances the capacity of his legs
to carry him at such speeds,
is chasing pigeons in the park
endlessly turning
to find a new pigeon.

Remarkably, they do not fly
but run on their little legs just
ahead of him as if understanding
perfectly this child's game.
He runs and runs, turning
to one pigeon after another.
There is nothing else in his world.

I scan the park and find
the grandfather, wisely,
like a grandfather, keeping
his distance, giving
this boy his rein, his realm.

Pneumonia

The lines of my face redrawn with a grime of urban dust
the coal-seam contrast of an Arbus image, I do not move
from the couch when they arrive to lug it into my lungs,

carefully setting one end in the left lobe, the other in the right.
The movers wait while I dig a few coins from my jeans, an effort
that causes a thudding in my chest. After they leave,

I protest that the world I've created does not comport
with this new arrangement. Back stage there is laughter;
when I angrily part the curtain there is a night more immense

than the edge of memory; a bone tossed there is never heard from,
a probe finds no other life, a needle pushed through the chest wall
to drain the fluid reports nothing, for better or worse,

but the grayness shown in scans, swelling slightly in a wind
across small northern seas where a dory rocks and a man stands
to hoist a sail. He hopes to reach land before nightfall but pauses

between each haul on the halyard, sweat gleaming on his face,
running down the black creases, almost like tears.

On Hearing the News
for Mark

Everything stops, except an instant
of wind that parts the drape.
Then everything goes on again,
imperceptibly changed, just as what was
simply your life, days ago
is history already tarnished by breath:

the boy in the woods,
woman in sunlight, someone
on a bicycle, crossing the bridge.
What next? Maybe we begin
reeling time back in, hoping to get
enough line on to change the past,

make something of all the conditionals
now permanent and there is an anguish
to this such that we must stop.

With all this in mind, I walk
into the large, gaudy room
marked NOW and find
there are tears in my eyes,

the simultaneous grief
and relief that comes
from knowing that this is
not the worst case, this

is not an end, but a difference
in the way life was, in about
a second or maybe less.

If I could turn and look back I'd see
this bend in things, the way old roads
moved left or right to accommodate
the immoveable, the moral, or just
the beauty of the curve.

Liminal

1.

My children grew up in a house
without thresholds
between door bottoms and floors
to impede the progress
of rodents and cold, keep
the chaff in the threshing room.

So when my toddling daughter discovered
the hard barrier with her staggering feet
she fell. The scar from those stitches
and the ills of the world
are there still. And from that moment
of betrayal her new life began
hurtling on its singular path
rising and falling like river winds.

I don't remember how we staunched
the bleeding or tried to soothe the pain
and shock, or that dreadful moment
between her sharp gasp and the wail of pain,
how long we waited before going
to the clinic for stitches. I imagine

the child on my knee as I hold an ice cube
inside wadded paper towels, softly
against her chin. I missed keeping that
in my memory, as we do, not seeing
those moments for what they are.
But I have it now.

2.

I can tell you my life's choices
were not decisions, paths taken,
but outcomes, a person, place or job
to which I drifted, an empty canoe
on an irresistible current. What did I learn
as the butcher at the beach store,
the reporter at the Upstate daily? How
did I get there or end up with this
person or that? In the house by the river
or the hovel where the snow blew in?

On the road crew I met the ex-con
whose quiet deliberateness would become to me
a way of being under the force of change.
From the podium of the classroom, I heard
the voice of the young immigrant son
telling stories better than any I had yet read
or written. On the beach with a dying man I saw
his vision beyond the veil he faced and felt
his conviction. So when I sat beside the lake
with the knowledge of what would kill me
and thought to ask only for peace,
I got it. I shifted then to another space
I am often tempted to leave but learned
to take with me, along with all the rest.

3.
On a path in deep woods we often come
to change, pure and simple, where
for reasons known to the trees alone
they change in type and hue and take the ground
with them in texture and rhythm. Or a wall
of stones piled long ago to make a field for crops
gives way to a path or woods road and we know
we've gone from some use to another but nothing more
except woods are like that and no one really
owns the land any more than time.

Sometimes we stumble and sometimes we fall.
Some doorways pass by us unnoticed
like the source of a sweet scent or slight music
we sense later but looking back cannot discover
what it was or ever find it again. Move on.
For whatever the moment is, whether
there is a memory or a lesson, it has no meaning
without the future, the chance to see
how it works, as if under our feet the world is moving.

At night the wind may be time rushing past the window.
Stand on the ground that is traveling a thousand miles an hour
and, if you can, feel a silence and hear a stillness, find a peace
that is real, a heart-serene space where your vistas
make sense and the music comes back to you
and even, for a moment the sweet scent,
on an airless wind. You cannot stay.

III

Genealogy

I'm looking for a man in a tweed jacket, rimless glasses,
white moustache and a fedora
that may have a feather in the band.
He might have a dog; he might have
a double-barreled shotgun open over his left forearm.
He may be smoking a Lucky Strike. He may be willing
to give you some direction otherwise unspoken.

Are there more things that we are not supposed to say
than there are things we are not supposed to hear?
Why would blood be a secret? Why were the troubles hidden
in novels instead of table napkins?
Were generations refused childhood, to do
what they'd never been taught?
What could be remembered by a soul
scorched by famine, war, famine, more war
that would be understood by a child kept captive
in a white world, cleaned and recleansed,
designed to shine so brightly
no memory could be seen?

> *The landscapes are all different, the accents, the rituals*
> *that sometimes suffice in the present but are incapable*
> *of sustaining the weight of generations, a heaviness*
> *accumulating as the lives, like that sudden flower*
> *of rocket fragments in blue sky, arc away*
> *from the stems of so many broken hours. Was I looking,*
> *or was my head already bowed, unable to utter a warning,*
> *to form a notion of the what or why that might*
> *have changed a trajectory before it was discovered*
> *the sky was made of tin and left-over smoke.*

I'd ask him what he did with the children
when there was nothing else to do, long before
anyone within earshot would think to wonder
what that would mean. I'd look closely
at the lines running from his eyes over his weathered cheeks;
see if they emerge from a smile, if I can get one

or if they are tear ditches, left from nights
of Scotch and regret, the only solution available
besides a dog and a gun and a field from which a bird rises.
Men watch its slow path until a blast
brings a burst of feathers and the dog
is sent out with a soft whistle.

So it's learned again. Sometimes the avid reader
may see the shape of things before getting to a precipice,
divergence of paths, request or seeming necessity.
On the dry street in the blue before sunrise, the last
newspaper page skips and hustles its rising and scraping
way along the wind, impossible to read. A radio
wakes someone or is still playing last night's music.

Apple Seed

1.
It was a long day on a long road,
straight through the cold November
dawn to dusk, measuring from pavement
to the height of land on the other berm
of the road-side ditch, every time
the foreman said "Here".

I'm sure we would have stopped
for coffee and for lunch, picking
a place to sit for dryness
or out of the wind that came
down off Ontario, cold as Canada,
but I only remember the end,

where we finished at an orchard
and there was one last apple
forgotten by the migrants or,
hanging alone, appearing
by some magic at that
unimaginable moment.

Regardless, I picked it
and lay on my back beneath the tree
and ate it, cracking with its coldness
and a juice so sweet and rich
I had to look again and again
to confirm its appleness

and at the end I gnawed close along
the stem to harvest every morsel
of this complete form of apple, every
succulent bit, drawing out the seeds
and spitting them upwards, watching
as they arced into the brown fall grass.

Warmed by the cold apple and my
own surrender to the fatigue

of all-day walking and bending,
closing my eyes, I dreamed
and all around me sprung up
apple trees in full blossom.

A little dream, seconds
only before I was wakened
to get in the truck
for the long drive back
crammed in with men smelling
of mud and cigarettes.

2.
At the end of some road
north toward the lake,
if you could find it, you
may come upon an orchard,
if it's not all houses now.

At the corner a little copse
of younger trees; their apples
the sweetest of any field.
Who are we to question
the possible, when a seed
so small can hold all

the green, the white and pink,
the gold and red
tumbling on as certain
as the sun's horizons?
What packed that gift,
and drew the ribbon, tight,

tighter, pulling all time
wisdom and beauty
into a bundle
so small
a man
could spit it in an arc?

I cannot argue
whether that dark seed,
pulled tighter, into the densest
point of all matter, everything we
have so far known or guessed,
was not ordained.

How close are we now
with our engineering
to the moment when
our cup will be ready
to accept all there is
and we prove infinite

the ability to shape
what is, what will be
and transcend our plane
just in time to realize
we should have known
enough to stop?

Hubble Ultra Deep Field Image

There, against the ultimate gloom
of what we do not know, is
the splattering of everything we do.

The whole place is littered
with tiny disks of whirling stars,
galaxies of millions of suns

and planets and moons
and every color of light in pinpoints
farther off than those

and then farther. All on black satin
or maybe it's nothing, appearing
as space, with the same consistency

as rooms at night, but darker.
We fumble through the threshold
thinking to find with a foot

or an outstretched hand
the thing that will bruise us
or trip us up, not imagining

that we are in it, swimming
in a consciousness beyond fathoms
beyond what we could have conjured

even as children, cautiously
entering the ocean at night
for the first time.

House of Mud and Water

There is the rain, the danger of sliding away.
The strangers, dripping brims of their hats pulled
low over dark eyes, coming in and out,
as if repossessing something, carrying

nothing, but leaving tracks on the floor.

One of them was apparently the dead man
though I couldn't tell him by his slouch,
gestures, nor a black suit
or pale johnny, both

common apparel in this crowd.

It seemed as if there was a train
judging by the occasional shaking,
deep rumbling, even a whistling
that built and subsided like a long scream

I never went to find. The children said

it was something else, but never what,
stuttering from their fetal curls.
They breathed like cats,
wheezing and whimpering

in dreams no one could diagnose.

Of course I learned to despise every breath,
all the well-inspected faults, the cracks
and little shreds of ancient grass or reed,
and the smell that lounged there, red eyed

as a night bird or a slug of memory.

It was all proof of what I suspected,
the lesson whispered, day upon day
upon night: no, no, no,

little things, a snarl of herded mice

always barring the path, guarding the door.

Empty

I want to write a poem
empty of you, a place
where there is not the scent
or sound of you,
no shadow in the air,
gray of distant rain, where you
have passed. But to do this

I have to squeeze it so tight, twist
it up hard like the towels kids snap at each other
late on the beach, dancing and shrieking
odd fairies not knowing they are
on the edge of love. But you see

even this does not work.
I have tried prayer: asked
that this be empty as the cup
left by the summer spigot, empty
as the bowl of the dried beech leaf,
empty as the pockets of my father's
coat, where I found only ash.
Empty as your promise.

Leftover Heart

Wrapped in bright red foil
on the floor under the driver's seat
one of the dark chocolate hearts
you gave me while pretending
it was nothing
these were just hearts
leftover from Valentine's Day
so it was cheap chocolate too
and you just don't like dark
so I got to be given
half a bag of hearts
by you and to pretend
to be fake touched
when really I was
but wondering why I wanted
you to be giving me hearts
because our hearts
were very far apart I thought
but now I know
that distance
is nothing for hearts.

Beside the Garden

We hear in the late afternoons of summer
the rumble of distant thunder
but see no cloud and wonder how long
before we must take cover

or if we will never see this rain
or just stay out, letting the first drops
splatter us like small, overripe fruit,
soaking our shirts....

We stand as the deluge fills
our eyes and ears, rills through our flattened hair,
into our mouths like kisses, like inspiration, moving
us into the house, out of wet clothes.

This is how to identify the language
of clouds, the intention of the lightning
that is the only light we need
beyond what comes faintly from our bodies.

The jagged bolt that crosses the sky
springs from such touches, tappings of a code
understood along the roots
curling for sustenance

in the soils of our bodies.
We learn to love the flower
of anything that grows, try to leave
everything that chance, without weeding.

But remember the fruit
rotted in darkness, the vine
choked, the flowers withered
by the swords of rye?

How can we be too careful?
Waste the heart's work
in hope of fairness

never intended by a nature

whose talons tear the tapestry we claim is beauty's curtain,
whose weight of rain leaves flowers in the mud?

Beloved

But you, beloved, are not in darkness.... 1 Thessalonians 5:4

...thankfulness brings you
to the place where the Beloved lives. Rumi, Mathnawi III

1.
On the green mountain rising to cloud above the rock blasted open
for the railroad, a shepherd seems to pursue his flock
though these sheep only have eyes for some greener, deeper place,
no intention concerning their herder. Only we, who watch, bring
meaning to what seems a synchrony, the many ahead of the one.

We think this is not the way it is with the Beloved,
the one pursued by many, the shepherd leading the flock.
This has nothing to do with numbers, with flocks.
This simile is false. Truer is the leopard that brings down
its prey, one-on-one. And there that analogy ends as well,

for the beloved does not consume, is not consumed
but fills the other with fire, a burning ignited over and over
upon parting, by agony quenched only when there is union again.
The beloved, loving, pursues and, having captured, is pursued,
the Oh and Zero rolling on, on, to the horizon.

2.
In the morning, you could see the carcass
from the back window in the kitchen, lying open
as if someone had smeared rouge on its belly.
It seemed glad, this former sheep, legs stiffly skyward
with a kind of glee or prelude to prayer.

We'd heard the yipping the night before
but thought the fence and dogs would discourage
coyotes—they always had. But now I wished
I'd gone out with the shotgun to bring the herd
into the barnyard and fire off a couple rounds.

We buried her right where she lay, scraping
scraps of her into the hole along with the bloody soil,
piled field stones over her, and stuck a stake down
with her name, Jasmine, written in red marker.
I'd been told not to name my sheep.

3
Primitive, the custom of thanking the prey
before consuming its flesh, of blessing it at "grace".
Wolves do not bother. Primitive is not wild; wild is beyond, before
anything we can conceive, but the beloved is there
in the movement of things, the true and utter grace

but only of the pursuit. Grace is lost in hunger.
The wolf, the cheetah, coyote lunge and tear and shred
and shake the meat to render it, spreading blood
and shards of flesh and hide in wild celebration,
rose petals and rice on the steps to the altar.

Having so loved, they leave, long tongues lashing gore
from their muzzles, moving not directly away, but circling slightly,
making arcs of remembrance, the beginnings of the new yearning,
of the return, the re-turn, coming again to the hunt, in agony and
    exaltation....

Tamalpais

Beyond the redwood-spired silhouettes
of the dark slopes, the lights
of the bayside cities gleam, orange necklaces
on the graceful black shoulders of the water.

Rising and falling with the breeze
above the shadows comes a woman's voice.
She is singing. At this distance
there is no music

solely the voice, almost enough to bring the tune,
for me to remember the words of this blues ballad,
torch recording, but slightly less perfect:
these blues touch and twist

until whatever of me has wings
drifts off, wavering hawk-like against the city-lit sky
to search the mountain's side
while this old man goes happily in to bed.

Catch and Release

1.
As I watch the fisherman working,
brief metronome of rod rising and going back
in the glowing mist of the morning river,
the line releases a sudden arc
of water drops that prism for a second in the sun.
Soon, his thumb across the ragged dorsal fin,
the fisherman works the hook
from the bony lip
while the gills blink their slow red eyes.

2.
I imagine the fish he returns to the river:
First still, relearning the water,
then a slow wag into the dark. Sometimes,
the hook gone too deep, I see a fish,
white side up in the current.
The fisherman turns away.
On the porch, before I go inside,
I rub a finger in the valley between
my chin and lower lip.

3.
Leaving the street light of the bridge
I see you turn, the line of your body twisting,
to look back, the motion, slowed
in memory, pushing one arm
away, hand open as if in a low wave or
ready to return to mine, just before
you dissolve into the thinning light.
I would never see that hand again.

Cellar Hole

From the foliage-spattered logging road
it is hard to see this, at first a different
rhythm of leaves, then a pattern of stones,
finally a cellar hole

wrapped around a heap of boulders and cracked brick
that held the hearth and orients me now
to see that the front of the house is what seemed,
from the line of the road, to be the side.

Looked at from the moss-strewn clearing
that was this family's yard, it takes shape
and rises before me, a perfect
5-over-4 colonial, attached barn ...

and vanishes again in the sunlight of this crystalline
fall day, as another year's yellowed beech leaves
flutter into the remains of a dream, a life-and-death shelter
and spread across the pastures now studded with trees
and the road filled with brightly clad Sunday hikers.

I wonder where in these woods the abandoned plowshare leans,
where the hayrake rests near a half-buried wall of stones
cleared by man and horse. Or was it all sold at auction,

the father standing off to the side of the crowd,
eyes examining the toe of one boot
as it slowly spreads the dirt, left and right,
while his wife and children wait in the wagon
for the trip down this road they will never come up again.

His youngest girl stares up into the blue
blue of the autumn sky and watches
the yellow twirl of a single beech leaf
as it makes its way to earth.

Summer Night

I am on my way home on a summer night,
the air a velvet sweater on the skin.

I am on my way home full of the good and bad
of the summer night that will last

no longer than the breath on the skin,
soft as the thought of night,
and the good and bad of going home,
knowing it will be so much less
perfect than a summer night when the air
will hold you, take away this knowledge.

I am on my way home when I see a boy and a girl
who I know instantly as a boy and girl

because their bodies have that bird-like quality
of boys and girls, their postures the gawky
innocence that only boys and girls this young
still have, their clothes the kind of effortlessness
only children's clothes are allowed. They are talking
furtively and I know instantly they are furtive

because they look to see if I am looking
and turn away when they see I am

and I know suddenly what they are
talking about and precisely the pressure
it exerts in their bodies and the scraping
impossibility of it also and how they will turn

away from each other and walk home
in the light sliding out of this summer night

and nothing at home will ever
be as good as it was again.

At the Fair

There are lots of things
spinning here, imitations
of galaxies, universes, mental states.
You and I walk the fairway
that tomorrow will be a muddied swath
through a trampled field, otherwise green.

I imagine the whole production
whirling, jangling, ringing, flashing
rising off the ground, slowly at first
then turning deliberately, pivoting
on its highest point, the Ferris wheel
and suddenly plunging off

into the deep blue-black sky
leaving a trail of calliope notes
glowing like embers twisting
above a bonfire, shrinking to
a single point of light and then
blink—gone.

I turn to tell you this
and you hand me an apple
as if to say you're sorry
there are no bumper cars
and this, sweet serpent,
will have to do. I do not

touch you, but take a bite
watching your eyes all the while
like a gentleman kissing a lady's hand.

Turquoise

I thought this would be
easy because the transition is
so clear. And it comes so
well equipped: proper noun, noun, adjective, modifier,
all of these in one glance, one sense of
substance, hard but also like soap,
a kind of air
rubbed into a solid state,
but also like something uncertain,
tentative as a lizard.

And there is so much history, so much
alchemy involved, plenty of silt in the corners
and culture in the way of things
rough woven and worn down
more by wind than God
and less by money than dirt,
the sun-burnished paint jobs
of crumbling desert pickups.
Somewhere in all of this, also,
there are eyes

that hold it like a curtain
in front of more tears
than all the lost rivers,
eyes rising up at me
the way wind rises off the sand,
carrying dust and shadow
and sage and dreams, hats....
Jewels fall like hail until it gets
warm in the mid morning.
Then they fall like tears again.

I can do nothing.
Really it's just a thief caught
half way through the window, a lover
still forming apologies, strategies for escape, children
with stuff on their fingers, looking down. It was caught

by heat and pressure; we can do this
with a sense of loss, a little chaos
kicking us up from the pillow. Pow.
Eventually, oceans and skies are the only places left.
I thought this would be
easy because the transition is so clear.

With Without

It is hard to tell if it is the snowfield
I face without you

or the swirling night I dream
empty of you

or the path I search for when I think of living
where you are not

or the sound of a song I hear
and you do not

or the distance into which I must continue
regardless of you

or the view from the height I may ascend to
and find you already gone

or the voice I will turn to
that is not yours

or the beat of time dancing on the wing
passing near you

or the breath I will lose at last
without sight of you

or just the sound of the rain
you will feel on your hand without me.

Tennessee Valley, Marin County

We descend like water
through the rising hills and tang of eucalyptus
toward the rumble of ocean
on a wind tearing wisps of fog over the headlands.
I walked this path so many times
with a tattered consciousness racing off
somewhere east. Now each fragrance
and pulse of wave and wind draws me deeper,
rift on rift, into these broken hills,
where the skip and flight of each sparrow
is the counterpoint to the steadiness of my mind,
harmony to the flutter and skitter
of the small bird of my heart,
skipping off ahead, yearning
for the thundering froth and sifting
on a beach so small
it can only be a gateway.

Girls on a Swing
for Lily

The old post-frame swing set
rocked on its back legs
as if it might gasp in upon itself
and fling the flying pink and blond
giggling sisters onto the mud
of the foot paths
dragged below their seats.

So I stopped pushing, watched
my daughters lying flat back,
hair streaming, legs stretched,
their tiny hands gripping the ropes,
as they arced through speckles
of sunlight and shadow cast
by the spring buds of the maple,

sawed and split and burned
winters ago now. I understand: I could not
spare those girls either sun or dark
but pray always that each discovers
the peace to tilt back laughing
in whatever light she finds.

When My Dead Father Called
after Robert Bly

It's a long story, but I was sleeping
between two couples,
in a shelter in the deep black
of the mountain night
when the phone rang.

I answered, and my father said
my name and I said "Dad"
and he said "You must wonder
what's going on when I've
left you alone so long."

I stared into the darkness
without hope of seeing anything
except my father's face, but nothing
was there except the blackness.
"Dad," I said. "Dad?" But the line

was dead and I was left with a longing
deeper than that silence
or the knowledge that there was
only the cold mountain air
and the soft sounds of the sleepers

in the down bags beside me.
There was no snow, and my father
sounded warm, as if he was calling
not from a street corner or wilderness
but perhaps from the living room

of the house where I last hugged him.
His voice was clear and steady
and he was right: I did wonder
because he had left me alone one time
that lasted years. He knew no better.

Mornings in the Heart

The birds, as usual, are busy
with their bird things. A rabbit,
rare visitor, weeds the lawn
between the woods and the lily bed.
The lake ripples with feeding
—turtles, fish or otters, it's hard to tell.
The loons continue various communiqués.

Elsewhere, a man kneels
before a fire, blowing gently
to revive last night's heat.
He is out of matches
and wants coffee and warmth
again, here in a forest
he knows not how deep.

In a far, far distance, I hear also
the whump and whistle of mortar
and rocket and "small arms" rattle.
I know there is hidden in that
the imperceptible cries of the wounded,
wails of the parents, sobs of the children,
in dust and rubbled homes,

who kneel also before flames.
In the woods, the man will keep
the fire burning as long as he can.

IV

Planting

When I put my hands in the dirt, push them
through the crumbling dampness as far
as they will go before time begins
to dig back under my nails, I reach inside—
beyond the world electrified and moving
in blurred lines of buzzing light
that altogether become a hiss—
there is a beating heart, a breathing
in a blackness where stars are allowed.

When I put my hands in the dirt, moving them
into the flesh of the planet, one pair
among millions, I stir a smoky potion
soaking a dry-hulled bundle yearning
into more life, turning and reaching for starlight.

When I put my hands in the dirt they are
like so many others linked to arms,
to elegant shoulders, the long curve
of muscled backs, all spreading
from seeds, those same earthborn bundles
holding all that we are: human, subject to love
and scorn, joy and death
and the feeling of all that, fleeting.

The Smuggler
for Eva

Grows his eyebrows out.
Crosses the shoulders, the clavicles
of mountains, the frontier, at dawn
carrying everything you want
on his back, the contraband
under his hat.

He tries to slide a tree bark
inscribed with the antidote
for insanity, banned years ago,
past the striped gate
of your eyelashes, praying
the hinges are not rusted.

He knows the guards, cousins
or the lovers of cousins. They ask
if he wants retsina, krupnik. He refuses.
He is working, after all, and his heart is busy
with the business of clouds, sliding bales
across boundaries you've wanted to believe in
for, what? Decades at least. Until this

coldness, at first a fog, drizzling
down your spine, then
a freshet of dread and compression
as if memory, something
that must not be forgotten,
bursts against your chest.

This is his work. Again
you find yourself in love,
out of love, smeared
with a grief that seemed
washed away, scrubbed.
Now the bridge is out, water

rises toward your knees.

Spaces

Think of the energy in the air between lips
parting slightly to receive a kiss!
Or the same lips closing after saying goodbye,
already turning away
along with the face so loved
that the eye on the other side of the space widening
closes also, almost catching the tear
that escapes in the instant
just under the lid crashing down, the closing
window that fills the body, makes it real.

Fail to understand these spaces and you are always
running too long, walking too late,
afraid of spinning: the only way to stay still
in a vastly moving vortex of straining stars!
Then the heart becomes a dented thing
finally left in a space in the woods
beside an old road, and the children
run through it, take anything of value,
which is to say all the shiny things,
though never merely, for it is still a heart: cleaned out
it becomes a dance hall, a garden.
People move in and out, choosing
what they want, dancing among the flowers
or the flowering fruit, and the music

weaves through the vines, gathers
a bouquet it lifts softly
to the space just above the closing lips
so that they stop, breathless,
for a moment long enough
to call those lips back, turn them,
lift the hand to the hand waiting, allow the space
between the bodies to close, the air rushing out,
wind through the canyon carrying a red dust
that anoints the faces of these lovers
who have made their rhythm one
and turn now slowly as a flower to the sun.

Straight Forward

On the branch
covered in ice
there is a sparrow
in the sunlight.
Your feet are cold
and just before I kiss
your cheek the smoke
of our breath mingles
in a single cloud.

In a Window

From down the road, there is just
the silhouette of the house, slumped
in the light of the moon and snow

and the orange star gradually
becoming a window and then a frame
where a man and a woman face one another,

standing. There is also a mirror
on a pine wall, blond in the light
of a lamp on the table behind them.

I see them from my car for an instant
in which the man raises his hands
to the woman's shoulders.

Peepers

His truck rattles down the road
like a bag of cans, banging
over the potholes
until a gear grinds and that
straight-six Ford whines down
as he slows against the engine,
rolls to a ticking stop.

The last indigo of day
silhouettes the still-bare trees.
In just enough light, he sees
the bright green shoots spiking out
from the pale stubble of last summer's reeds
jumbled along the edges of the pond.
He leans on the fender,

and listens. Closes his eyes,
lifts his head slightly
as if picking up some fragrance
or recalling something distant. He is still.
Around him, the sound grows
until it is thick as the air
congealed ghost-like above the pond.

Motionless, he rises on the pulses,
the threads and seesaws of sound,
a syncopation so perfect it weaves the carpet he rides
past years and roads and rocks, feet shuffling
over thresholds, birds and children singing,
sunlight crossing water, the warm back
of a wooden chair in winter.

He enters a room without regret, where
a woman stands smiling, lifting her arms.

The Last Weekend in the Country

following the announcement of the supposed discovery
of the identity of the "Dark Lady" of Shakespeare's sonnets

It is Saturday night. He stares at the paper,
wondering if the smooth olive skin,
the robust blossoming of beauty's
"successive heir" is worth the time, the lost
characters and forgotten rhymes....

Emelia sits by the fire. She picks at needlepoint—
again they have quarreled because he hates beans—
so that when, reminding her of more
heated exchanges under this thatched roof, he holds up
twenty-five or so sonnets as proof,

she says "You're a genius." And goes in to bed.
Saying nothing, he blows out his candle and
goes out, walking on the bank by the cool,
dark river, to give new lines to his favorite fool.

History

Of course there are clouds, and birch trees
bending deer-like, as if drinking the snow.

There are berries as red as a skinned knee
bright as blood beads glimmering
against the scraped-white skin
of the snow-filled sky.

If a dog barks, others howl in a distance made uncertain
by the hair rising on the back of your neck

as if hair is responsible for perception
and there were a way to forget the way my fingers

swept the hair from the back of your neck
or the way your eyes closed slowly or the way I grew wings
just before the treeline or the way there was suddenly
a complete absence of clouds or sound or air.

In the End

She was not even
a camp survivor
but a pile of bones
draped with a sheet,
a snow-covered range of peaks,
shoulder, elbow, hip and heel.

Only small places moved:
her eyes, a pulse of skin
below one ear, and the drum
of breath that throbbed
between the tendons
at the front of her neck.

On the phone they said her breathing
was shallow, but it seemed to me
deeper than ever, drawing the skin
back into her throat with its will
just to go on bringing the air
into her body, to feel, at least, that.

Her eyes had gained a distance
years before; in photographs
you could see this about her,
that her body no longer paid attention
to the world, seemed instead to shrug,
preoccupied with some longer vista.

In the end, her eyes cleared and looked
in to me, seeing everything
I had not bothered to hide:
resentment's cauldron, the skin of bitterness
stretching over the shoulder of forgiveness.

The Wave

My father waved me away
the night before he died
the way the policeman
gestured the crowd back
just before the walls curled in
and the collapsed church
rose in a flower of flame
followed by a billion
tiny orange lights
crazing the whole black sky.
And we, my father and I
and a hundred others
who had lined the pew rows,
passing candlesticks and crosses,
hymnals and cushions, out
to the storm-cooled safety
of that summer evening,
stood and lost our breath
in the blush of heat
when the roof
and the walls
fell in. Then there was
just the hiss and pop
and the thrum of the engines
and the stars coming back
one by one.
I think my father
put his hand
on my shoulder. I don't
remember if he cried
with everyone else.
He may have chosen
to spare me that
when he could,
saving the wave
for the time
when he could not.

The Woodsman

An enchanted forest is an easy place
for a heartless, inedible fellow.
I'd never a care a Brillo bath and a few
shots from an oil can couldn't cure.
Life was simple: see a tree, cut it down.
My evenings were spent rattling around
from stack to stack, counting.

That was before the rain.

Slowly, soundless as time, it grew to mist;
I was already going stiff before I heard
the pattering on my funneled pate
like bees when I've made a bad choice of tree.
By then, it was too late; the can out of reach, the joints
grinding tighter, until that final Pompeiian moment....
You spend a few decades standing
stock still, with an ax frozen
over your head and it makes you think.

So, by the time the girl showed up,
I was ready. Of course, if I'd known
what life was going to be like afterward,
I might have told her to spare the oil
and leave me thinking. Not to mention
I'd stand in the woods forever
just to miss those monkeys!

But as luck would have it, I got a heart.

Once in the boiler of my tin chest a thought
echoed like a boy shouting in a cistern,
round and round and down and down
until dying in a whisper. Now there's a cauldron
where musings are heated into notions,
whose fumes rise to warp and spin
in the crazy winds of passion. Suddenly
I see things in a long and lovely light, wish

I knew the words to songs, and lie
awake at night, with the anguish of the lover, poised
above, but not quite ready for, a dream.

Children

Standing before a bench
in the small town park,
the man clasps the handle
of a stroller where his son
is about to begin crying.

Ribbons of sunlight cross the damp grass,
snake up the trunks of maples
along the blue, stone-dust paths.
One touches the man's leg
but he cannot move. At night now

he hears things flying
in the woods, tries to answer
but only dreams of falling. If he is lucky,
his skin will rise off him, a shroud
revealing the boy left bargaining in prayer.

Flooded

The huge yard of my childhood seemed small when I went back
to the old neighborhood. My father'd mapped that full acre of lawn
into plots I could handle with the big reel mower, each section
assigned a price of pennies for my allowance—a way of teaching
me to see the insurmountable as a series of smaller steps.

The mower handlebars reached my throat, rubber-capped
grips splaying out to my shoulders, throttle control on the left,
on the right the lever that engaged the blades and wheels.
I quickly learned to hang on tight and ease the throttle forward
once the machine was in gear so it wouldn't drag me to the ground.

Often unable to pull the starting cord with force enough
to make the Briggs and Stratton catch, I turned it over
and over 'til the sweet tang of gasoline told me
the engine was flooded and I'd have to wait before I could
even try to start it again. I'd pace, then, conscious

that each passing minute kept me from the game starting
at the ball field down the street and how I'd miss a whole game
if enough other kids showed up—knowing if I tried to pull that cord
too soon I'd lose more time. It was an exercise in self control, marching
back and forth pounding the ball in my glove, smelling neatsfoot, gas,

and the sunbaked dust of the ball field. Today is opening day
of my 71st baseball season, memory trailing back to Williams, Parnell
and Piersal, Jackie Jensen, Eddie Joost. Spring is pressing its light
hard on the frozen ground, raising crocuses in sun-soaked corners
flooding me with smells, bird sounds, the distant callings
of boys on diamonds and the flick and click of my father's Zippo
at the end of a summer day when we'd sit on the brick terrace
he with a Schlitz and a smoke I matched with Coke and Cracker Jacks,
with Curt Gowdy's play-by-play, the smell of the beer
and sweat and mown grass. And so flooded, I cannot start

either to move to what it is or was I had thought to do today,
the small chores of an older man, a walk in the woods
with the dog, older too and slow, or turning to reach

the next book from the side table in the sun beside my reading chair. I have to stop and wait in this coming back of so much life, revel rather than pace, sink down into it and wait while it passes slowly taking time with it, but not time that is lost.

Sugar Maples

The closest is straight and so the tallest.
The next is slightly bowed and split.
The last, curled as a question mark.
Each holds proudly its quiver of branches
and under the sky, there is no
first or last in this line of sweet utility,
and doubtless the taste of one
could not be discerned different
from its siblings' by any palate.

But let me tell you:

that the bent and shortest tree stands
as near the sky as the others
because of its place highest
on the sloping field and farthest east
and you may see the difference—

how this tree is first,
having taken the wind off the faces of its sisters;

how this tree is most hurt, most lonely;

how in carrying its face to the wind
all the long, howling night it must have been unsure
if those it shields were there at all,

or if their fiber might have failed
and the sound of their leaving
been carried off in the wind;

how this tree is bent within and tempered
in a way greater than any we can see.

Moving O'Keeffe

On a high-end Manhattan avenue, police
close a lane for our truck at the curb; escorted
six floors to an apartment big as half a city block,
parquet floors, Persian rugs, tapestries and blank
spaces on richly textured walls where the paintings
we will move had hung. Nestled now in custom cases,
glass tops covered by satin, their nature and beauty
hidden. I am dazzled, the one-day help for a friend
on a short-handed mission to a world plush and dense,
the air softer, more breathable.

I am not to know these people, who stand
and smile with a casual friendliness at once alert, nor
what it is I wear white gloves to move.
Grasping the handles of a case, itself a work of art,
I am led carefully to the street, where two others
pack the boxes in the truck.

A little wind moves up the avenue, a sudden gust kicks
dust into my eyes: I wince against the city sand,
stand frozen, blind, afraid to move with the art
in my hands. When at last I open my eyes, just
as the box is taken from me, an orchid is revealed,
large, alive, it moves for an instant, vibrancy
shaking every sense—

light streams through the tall windows of a classroom
wind scrapes around the weathered corners of a desert house
a figure disappears darkly into a landscape—

and then the coverlet, flipped off by the breeze
that must have moved the painted petals,
is smoothed back in place, the flower
gone into the truck.

Saving the Lilies

Who knows how long ago some soul, fond
of the bright explosions of daylilies,
sunk a blade into the clay marl beside the pond
to bury deep the dull orange tubers I now unearth.
This pool of lilies for long summers bloomed
holding the bank, blocking the flow of fertilizer
and pesticide robbing fish and frogs of breath.
This year the battle of men against what seems
the chaotic will of nature rumbled up to this front:
the groundsman decreed the lilies be mowed
to perfect the swath of lawn down to the shore.
But I've managed a compromise in the face
of pristine progress: a lily preserve, into which I herd
the unruly offenders; short-handled shovel
as my shepherd's crook, I unearth those clumps
outside the reservation, the blade crunching
through the carrot-like roots of the outermost.
Inside the cordon, I open a pit, water, and slosh
the newly arrived amongst their siblings.
My friend Tom comes and takes the stragglers
to plant a family of Maine cousins; we wedge them
into plastic bags and put them in his truck.
When we're done, the lilies hold a tight oval,
roped off from the mowers ridden by young men
in headsets and mirrored sunglasses.

Pine Bluffs

Two farmers, giant machines thrumming
across thatched fields of corn stubble,
play whack-a-mole with lightning fires we watch
from the porch of the Stuckey's, happy for hot coffee
and sticky buns, ours having recently been dragged
from drowning in a flashed-out culvert under
the Lincoln Highway where we sheltered from the storm
until the epiphany—this is the water's way, not ours—
launched us, packs jostling as we sprinted the half mile
along 30 to this shelter, rain spraying us like shot, thunder
roaring around us as the storm blew east across a prairie
of smoke and dust and weeds, fire erupting
where spears of light threaded down as if a cartoon God
chased a road-running demon—or demons,
perhaps Jim and me, transported from under a bridge
in Hardin, Montana by a cuckold from Butte with a big truck,
a case of beer, heartache and a shotgun. We'd lied our way
onto the shoulder in Sheridan, to be plucked by a preacher
who'd seen Jesus in a peach tree in Wichita; he warned
400 thousand Japanese on flying Kawasakis were coming
"with a rattling and a crashing" (Romans, chapter and verse:
"Motorsickles; what else could it be?") and left us howling
and rolling on the breakdown lane in Cheyenne where we
spent the night in the railyard, sharing with hoboes stories
of the road made better by the bottles we passed.
No eastbound freights the next day, the drifters said,
so we took a bus to Pine Bluffs, walked out to the I-80 ramp,
where a trooper explained that things were different for long-hairs
in Wyoming, and we'd better get on the west-bound side of
the Lincoln Highway and walk to Bushnell, Nebraska,
if we didn't want to stay as guests of the Cowboy State.

Coralville

Along the straight highway through the stubbled fields,
the Rock Island freight crew climbs the snowy hill
to the motel coffee shop where they will order
jelly omelets, toast white, coffee black.

The waitress ignores the faint aroma of metal and sweat,
a mist rising in the heat off their Dickies as she pours the coffee,
swirling steam into mugs the men grip with two hands, warming
fingers burning with cold. Behind them, down the slope,

their diesels thrum on the siding, waiting for the Southwest Chief
to thunder past, headed for Kansas City, her passengers sipping coffee,
contemplating the horizon, the flatness of the empty prairie,
the long freight blurring by. Then the crew stands from their stools

with the slow stiffness of working men. Cash on the counter,
plenty of tip, cups drained of coffee, they zip bulky parkas and head
out the door. The waitress clears the counter, scooping bills and coin
into the bib around her waist, clutches the coffee pot and moves

down the line, waving the steaming vessel like a semaphore, filling cups
and clearing empty plates. Later, she'll pour coffee for truckers,
construction workers, linemen, some who know her name and some
who only tip their caps. 3:30, the long sun slanting in the back windows,

she empties the last pots, takes her tips and says goodnight to the cook.
Outside, a slight snow wavers in a west wind. Pulling her coat closed,
she fishes for her keys as she crunches across the parking lot.
A mile down the road, she parks at a small cape. In the kitchen,

a man stands at the table, raises his coffee cup for a last drink just before
she hugs him, reaching up to kiss him on the cheek, catching his smile
in the darkened window above the sink. Soon he will leave for second
     shift,
heading out to the pickup with his lunch pail and thermos of coffee.

About Bill Burtis

A native New Englander, Bill Burtis is a graduate of Hobart College and the Writers' Workshop at The University of Iowa. He now lives in Exeter, New Hampshire and Readfield, Maine, with the poet Nancy Jean Hill. *Liminal* is his first full-length collection of poems.